SHORTCUT OF ACCOUNTING SOFTWARE

KABIR DAS

Made with ♥ on the Notion Press Platform
www.notionpress.com

Contents

1

What is accounting software?

Accounting software manages and records the day-to-day financial transactions of an organization, including fixed asset management, expense management, revenue management, accounts receivable, accounts payable, subledger accounting, and reporting and analytics. A complete accounting system keeps track of an organization's assets, liabilities, revenues, and expenses. These transactions then populate the general ledger in real time, providing CFOs, treasurers, and controllers immediate access to real time, accurate financial data. It also allows P&L owners visibility into their performance at the operational level.

The systematic recording of these financial transactions enables the production of quarterly and annual financial statements, including balance sheets, income statements, statements of cash flows, and statements of stockholders' equity. Accounting software is a key component of an enterprise resource planning (ERP) system.

ERP systems unify essential business functions, such as accounting, financial planning and analysis (FP&A), supply chain, inventory management, and procurement. These applications are natively integrated with a common user interface and data model, eliminating the need to move between systems or integrate siloed data to manage different aspects of your business.

Industry's best accounting software ERP software

Benefits of accounting software

- Accounting software is crucial in helping organizations run their day-to-day business processes. It allows business leaders to keep their finger on the pulse of their company's financial health.

General ledger (GL) and subledger

- Modern accounting software is designed to allow both journal entries and automated subledger entries to automatically populate the general ledger, allowing CFOs and controllers to have a real-time view of their financial data.

Accounts payable (AR) and accounts receivable (AR)

- A complete accounting software solution does more than just basic accounting. It helps organizations to reduce records redundancy, deliver better budgeting and forecasting, and enable a thorough and properly categorized expense management. In addition, it provides seamless integration into banking systems, enables more accurate audits, and keeps detailed tracking records of all assets and liabilities.

Cash management

- The cash management capabilities in accounting software provide accurate cash positions by automatically reconciling cash transactions to bank statements. These capabilities also enable companies to make timely investing, borrowing, and other cash decisions with automated cash forecasting based on payables, receivables, payroll subledgers, and external transactions.

Asset management

- A modern accounting solution helps you manage the entire financial cycle of assets, including acquisition, capitalization, depreciation, and retirement. Having this complete visibility helps businesses deliver accurate financial statements related to appreciation and depreciation.

Risk management and compliance

- The best defense an organization has against fraud and unauthorized user access is accounting software with built-in security, risk management, and audit controls. These internal controls and separation of duties (SoD) help you stay compliant with Sarbanes-Oxley (SOX) regulations and give your enterprise a secure, single source of truth for data.

Collections management

- Managing collections involving customers is an important accounting software capability. With comprehensive collections management, it is easier to rank customers, establish collection strategies, manage collection payments, and initiate late-stage collections for bankrupt customers.

Revenue management

- Embedded revenue management capabilities in accounting software automate the process of using analytics to maximize revenue and profitability.

Reporting and analytics

- A complete accounting system not only records financial transactions, it also includes reporting and analytics capabilities. These prebuilt dashboards help finance leaders make sense of their organization's financial health and drill down for more detailed information. These dashboards measure critical financial KPIs in real time, including current ratio, quick ratio, debt-to-equity ratio, net working capital, and inventory turnover—just to name a few.

Accounting software—on premises or in the cloud

Since the introduction of accounting software nearly 45 years ago, it has evolved tremendously, from an on-premises deployment model to a cloud-based one. The first generation of accounting software was deployed on-premises, meaning the hardware and servers for the software were located in a company's datacenter.

Today, there is an increasing demand for cloud-based accounting software. When accounting software is "in the cloud," it simply means that the application runs on a network of remote servers instead of at a company's location.

The cloud offers a more affordable alternative for accounting software that lowers both operating expenses (OpEx) and capital expenditures (CapEx) because it eliminates the need for companies to purchase hardware or hire additional IT staff. With no costly infrastructure to support, resources can be invested toward innovation opportunities, while employees can focus on more strategic activities instead of managing IT.

There are four core operational concepts that are driving the move of accounting software from on-premises to the cloud. They include:

Eliminating upkeep

- Legacy software systems require a lot of maintenance from staff and consultants. These systems constantly need bug fixes, patches, upgrades, and maintenance fees. With cloud-based accounting software, the heavy lifting of tracking, diagnosing, installing, and testing fixes shifts from customer to vendor. Instead of having you work continually to fix the system, the system continually works for you.

Avoiding expensive maintenance

- On-premises software requires a great deal of time, effort, and money just to keep it running. With cloud-based accounting software, upgrades, disaster recovery, hardware refreshes, and backups are all handled as part of the service.

Real-time, accurate financial data

- Accounting software solutions of the past often were designed to "batch transfer" transactions from subledgers to the general ledger. Cloud-based accounting software automatically posts all transactions to the general ledger, ensuring that the GL always contains real-time data.

No more shelfware

- The old practice of buying extra licenses for future users and potential projects ends with modern accounting software. With the cloud's SaaS subscription model, companies use the licenses they need and add more users or products as they grow.

The future of accounting software

Accounting software has evolved to meet the demands of a digital world, and the cloud has been key to this transformation. The cloud has elevated back-office accounting software to a comprehensive, mission-critical, integrated solution designed for innovation. As companies encounter new disruptive forces and competitive pressures, these agile, adaptable cloud accounting systems can enable them to achieve financial strength for the future.

Having a modern, cloud-based accounting software solution helps organizations compete in a digital economy. These comprehensive solutions include the following capabilities:

Advanced reporting and analytics

- Gain a comprehensive view into your organization's financial performance and better understand profitability, costs, and revenue by conducting historical trend and variance analyses using prebuilt metrics.

Next-generation technologies

- Modern, cloud-based accounting applications are often embedded with next-generation technology, such as artificial intelligence (AI), blockchain, machine learning (ML), and digital assistants.

Automation

- Built-in account reconciliation and transaction matching allows organizations to dramatically speed the financial close process. Learn how Oracle achieved the fastest close on the S&P 500—in just nine calendar days.

Lower total cost of ownership (TCO)

- The cloud eliminates the need for businesses to invest in hardware, maintenance, shelfware, and upgrades. Thanks to the speed and scale afforded by SaaS, organizations that use cloud accounting software experience a total cost of ownership that's up to 52% less (PDF) than on-premises customers.

Extreme scalability

- As companies grow, their financial management software must have the ability to rapidly and easily scale—across markets, geographies, and products. The data centers of cloud accounting software providers are engineered in a way that provides unmatched speed, performance, security, and scale.

Work from anywhere

- Cloud accounting software allows accountants, controllers, treasurers, and CFOs to access the application on any mobile device with an internet connection, from laptops to smartphones, enabling finance departments to work securely from anywhere, anytime, on any device.

Quarterly update cycle

- Oracle's software comes with automatic quarterly updates, enabling customers to take advantage of increased automation and more features—every 90 days.

A complete financial management suite

- We deliver the most comprehensive financial solutions available with applications for core accounting and finance, risk management, direct and indirect procurement, and project portfolio management (PPM).

Disaster recovery

- The security protocols embedded in cloud accounting software are far more extensive and modern than on-premises systems. Cloud providers regularly back up your data to servers in multiple locations, reducing the risk that a fire or natural disaster could compromise your instance of the system and information.

Compliance standards

- Today's organizations need more than a digital version of bookkeeping with spreadsheets. Beyond just recording transactions, cloud-based accounting software helps finance teams maintain their fiduciary stewardship, reduce accounting errors, shorten invoicing cycles, comply with ever-changing tax laws and regulatory requirements, and optimize cash flow.

Risk management

- As money is tracked and managed across the organization, accounting systems should help protect critical data against theft, fraud, and other criminal mischief. Cloud-based financial management solutions include risk and compliance management, so companies can leverage these capabilities beyond audit trails and error checks to include the separation of duties (SoD) and mapping of roles to responsibilities across the enterprise.

Cloud accounting is no longer just the future—it's something businesses need to adopt now to avoid operating at a competitive disadvantage. The benefits of cloud accounting software are similar to other cloud applications, but are even more crucial because financials form the basis for everything a business does. Running a company without accurate and real-time financial information is like driving a car without a speedometer or fuel gauge. That's why a cloud-based accounting system is such a critical investment for businesses today.

2

The Best Accounting Software In India (With Features)

To succeed, an organisation typically tracks its finances. There are a lot of accounting software platforms, but they may not all offer the same abilities for the same price. It is essential to find accounting software that fits your needs so you can perform tasks, like invoicing and payment acceptance, that benefit the company. In this article, we share a list of 21 of the best accounting software in India, with explanations of their features and uses.

Best Accounting Software In India

Knowing what the best accounting software in India is, can help you keep track of the finances of the company for which you work. Accounting software automates some accounting tasks and can keep records of a company's revenue and spending. This can help accountants and other finance professionals complete their work more efficiently. Here is a list of some of the most popular accounting software that professionals use in India:

1. Tally

Tally is a popular software among small businesses and accountants. It has multiple versions of the application to appeal to a wide range of users. Tally functions as an end-to-end solution to statutory regulations. Its top features include:

- Invoice and ledger creation
- Cheque printing
- Instant reports
- Automatic bank reconciliation
- Cost estimates
- Analysis of profits

2. Marg

Marg is a taxed-based accounting software that offers advanced features for businesses within the pharmaceutical and manufacturing industries. This application is also ideal for growing businesses that are preparing to e-file their taxes. Some of the top features Marg offers include:

- Automatic bank reconciliation
- Online payment system
- Companies can manage their business from a single platform
- GPS tracking application
- Mobile application to integrate orders and inventory
- Cloud-compatible versions available

3. Busy

Busy is an accounting software with three primary versions that businesses can choose from to best suit their needs. This application also offers both single-user and multiple users, which makes it a good option for both small and larger-sized companies. It offers special features for companies in industries such as manufacturing, retail, trading and distribution. Busy's top features include:

- Bill generation and printing
- Automatic GSTIN validation
- Automatic reconcilation

- Annual GST summary
- Inventory and stock management
- Cloud compatibility

4. Intuit QuickBooks

Intuit QuickBooks is a popular option for freelancers and small and mid-sized businesses. Quickbooks offers different products and pricing to fit the business needs of your employer. Its top features include:

- Time tracking
- Inventory recording
- Payroll processing
- Integration with payment software platforms like PayPal and Square
- Live bookkeeping
- End-of-year tax report
- 24/7 chat support

5. Zoho Books

Zoho Books provides simplicity in its accounting software. Many businesses rely on it to manage their accounting tasks and organise transactions. Its top features include:

- End-to-end accounting
- Tax compliance
- Mobile app
- Inventory tracking
- Time tracking
- 50+reports including profit and loss, inventory summaries and sales tax reports
- 14-day free trial

6. ProfitBooks

This accounting software is fully online and free for single users. This budget-friendly software is helpful for start-up companies and individuals who are preparing for taxes and managing financials. ProfitBooks is an advanced accounting platform that is user-friendly with a high-quality and easy-to-navigate website. ProfitBooks' top features include:

- Expense tracking
- Invoice creation
- Inventory management
- Tax record generation
- Inventory flow tracking
- Ability to create multiple warehouses

7. Logic

Logic is an enterprise research planning (ERP) software that caters to distribution, retail and manufacturing companies. This software can help track business expenses and inventory. Here are some of Logic's top features:

- Ledger integration
- Sales forecasts
- Human resources, accounting and inventory management
- Taxation management and auditing
- Collaboration tools
- Document sharing
- Workflow management

8. myBooks

myBooks by Zetran is a cloud-based accounting software that provides its users with a lot of security, which is especially important because myBooks connects to your bank and imports your transactions. Its top features include:

- Create invoices

- Statements in easy-to-read graphs and charts
- Templates
- Simple configuration
- Analytical dashboard
- 24/7 support via chat

9. Vyapar

Vyapar is a free application for invoicing, inventory and accounting for businesses. This application is well suited to small and medium-sized companies. Vyapar's key features include:

- GST compatibility
- Automatic backup of files
- Free trial for premium features
- Availability on mobile applications and PCs
- Automatic payments
- Contact business insight monitoring
- Invoice creation and printing

10. Saral

Saral is an accounting software that helps small businesses completely monitor their finances, inventory and service and billing. The application is popular among several industries, including retail, distribution and timber. Some of Saral's key features include:

- Service invoicing
- Stock reports
- Mobile application integrations
- Ability to sync data from mobile websites
- Alerts for live stock updates
- E-payment extract

11. Realbooks

Realbooks collects and stores financial data so businesses can make better decisions. It is an online platform that is GST compliant and a resource for businesses to complete accounting, payroll and inventory tasks. Here are some of the key features Realbook offers:

- Document management
- API integration
- Flexible bill analysis
- Manual bank reconciliation
- Real-time data management
- Receipt and payment advice generation
- Sale and purchase reports

12. Reach

This software caters to small and medium businesses. Reach bundles all business operations into one application, which can help businesses view and analyse data in a convenient, organised and efficient manner. It has powerful business automation software that can effectively manage multiple accounts at once. Its top features include:

- Customised invoices
- Email and website lead captures and management
- Import options
- Inventory management
- Cloud-compatibility
- End-of-day reporting
- Custom-made for your business needs

13. Zipbooks

Zipbooks is an online accounting software for businesses that want to operate on the go. There is a free option, but for a fee, you can upgrade to a version that includes bookkeeping. Some of its top features include:

- Invoicing
- Automated billing
- Payment reminders
- Intelligent reporting
- Online payments colour-coded for ease of use

14. Alignbooks

Alignbooks is a cloud-based accounting software that you can also access offline. It is ideal for small and medium-sized businesses. Some of Alignbook's top features include:

- Secure data backup
- Bill generation
- Built-in operational controls
- Flexible deployment

15. ZenScale

ZenScale is a cloud-based enterprise resource planning accounting software for small and medium-sized businesses. ZenScale offers custom pricing, which allows companies to choose the plan that best suits their needs. ZenScale's top features include:

- Real-time visibility of business transactions
- Control system for scheduling and inventory
- Payroll management software
- Automatic GST reports
- Mobile application availability
- Tax preparation

16. Bench

Bench is an accounting software that mostly focuses on taxes. If you work for or own a small business and want to make sure you are ready for tax season, then Bench may be the ideal option for you. Bench works by turning your financial statements into data that is ready for tax filing. Some of its top features include:

- Bookkeeping team that imports bank statements and prepare financial statements
- Year-end package with everything you require to file your taxes
- Ability to work with your CPA
- Monthly financial statements
- Mobile app

17. BookKeeper

BookKeeper is a GST accounting application catered to businesses within the industries of retailers, wholesalers, distributors and manufacturers. This application allows users to access it both from their mobile devices and desktops. BookKeeper's top features include:

- Data synchronisation across users and platforms
- Customisable invoice templates
- Free updates
- Inventory management
- E-commerce integration

18. Wave

Wave cloud-based software that is easy to use for business owners with no accounting or bookkeeping experience. It is a wonderful option for businesses who are on a budget as it offers a free version. Its top features of the free version include:

- Tracking of transactions
- Receipt scanning
- Invoice management
- Offers a paid monthly subscription if you need payroll processing

19. Xero

Xero is a great option for businesses that intend to grow. While most accounting software charges per user, Xero allows you to add more users as you add people to your team who need access to Xero without a price change, and it is cloud-based. Some of its top features include:

- Inventory tracking
- Recurring invoices
- Track projects
- Multi-currency accounting
- Online and PDF quotes
- Integrations with 700 different apps
- 24/7 support via email and live chat

20. Kashoo

Kashoo has branded itself as the world's simplest accounting software. Kashoo is ideal for freelancers and businesses with fewer yearly transactions. Some of its top features include:

- Unlimited number of users
- Income and expense tracking
- Categorisation of debits and credits
- Automatic reconciliation
- Online invoice payments
- Connection to bank accounts
- Collaboration features with other accountants and bookkeepers

21. FreshBooks

FreshBooks combines a lot of the features that accountants, small business owners and accounts clerks require to complete their work. It uses cloud-based software, making it easy to access on mobile phones and desktops. Its top features include:

- Highly intuitive invoicing tools
- Recurring invoices
- Most functions available on a single dashboard
- Mobile app

- Organised expenses
- Automatic deposits
- Easy to access customer support

Hope this list of best accounting software in India helps you in selecting the most appropriate one for your employer.

3 Tally

Tally ERP 9 shortcut keys make your Tally accounting work faster, simpler, and easy. Tally ERP 9 accounting software is known for easy-to-use and convenient Tally function keys. Tally ERP shortcut keys enables users to use their Tally account easily and more efficiently. Tally when hosted on Cloud perform 10x better. Tally prime on cloud or Tally on Cloud benefits organization and even single user. Download Complete list of Tally shortcut keys in pdf format from the below form.

Knowing Tally ERP 9 all shortcut keys is the best solution to boost your speed. Tally ERP 9 shortcut keys are primarily used to enter fast transactions and cut down our efforts. Tally shortcut keys list can used to operate, analyze, and report the financial statements. Shortcut keys in Tally ERP 9 enable users to analyze the statements for fast decision making.

What is Tally ERP?

1. Tally ERP 9 is an admired software for enterprise resource planning used by professionals.
2. They use Tally for handling company's accounting, inventory control, order management, tax management, payroll, banking, and many other specifications.
3. All day-to-day processes are supported by the application, from tracking invoices to creating different MIS reports.

4. The newest version of Tally, which was released in 2009, is Tally ERP 9.
5. Tally short keys provides a range of features for small and large businesses.

What do you mean by using shortcut keys in Tally ERP application?

The attention is drawn to list of keyboard shortcut keys for Tally ERP 9, as shortcut keys in Tally ERP 9 software utilizes the keyboard functionality to run, journalize, and record the financial statements generated for the users. Tally function keys helps via the financial statements to take fast decisions.

The keyboard shortcut key is about a series of one or more keys that can be used to trigger a function without touching a mouse. As a substitute to mouse clicks or contentious usage Enter Key. Tally ERP 9 shortcuts can trigger any command in this application.

There is a list of shortcuts for practically all functions in Tally ERP 9. Tally keyboard shortcuts allow to access the program without using the mouse. Tally shortcut keys list will facilitate you in speedy data entry, quick navigation, easy processing of reports, easy printing, data export-import, etc.

Conclusion:

The Next Chapter mentioned list of Tally all shortcut keys including shortcut keys in Tally GST could be helpful to users. Tally shortcut key help in using your Tally account easily and with pace. Tally ERP 9 all shortcut keys can be used for any business operations. If you want your Tally to be more effective and want to remote access Tally on Cloud for Mac or any devices, you can reach us at Tallystack.in. We at Tallystack offer affordable Tally on Mac or Tally prime on Cloud or Tally Cloud price.

What are combination shortcut keys in Tally ERP 9?

For menu navigation in the Tally application, these are the most effective shortcut keys. You may have realized some of the letters in the menu are bold in red color. If this red-letter is pressed, you'll be directed to that menu by the tally.

For instance, To generate a GST report, the shortcut key combination is as below:

D > O > G from the TALLY GATEWAY and GST REPORT MENU will be on the screen.

How to get started with Tally on cloud?

We'll get you coated as we are offering you an idea of how to get started with it.

1. Firstly, start with browsing through our Tallystack website.
2. Secondly, as per your requirements get your tally on cloud server configured by contacting us.
3. Thirdly, you can operate the Remote desktop client (RDP) from devices like Windows, Linux, Mac, or Android.

After your Tally on cloud is registered, one of our officials will assist you and our experts will provide your Tally on Cloud IP address, Domain name (usually set as your company's name), and administrator login/ password.

4

Tally Shortcut With GST

Shortcut Keys in Tally ERP 9

1. **F1=Select or open the company using this key.**
2. **Alt + F1=To see the constrained messages, use this shortcut key to select the inventor.**
3. **Ctrl + F1=This key could be used for selecting a payroll voucher from the Accounting screen or Inventory voucher.**
4. **F2=To change the date.**
5. **F3=Tax Properties and selecting the company for selecting the corporate statutes.**
6. **F4=For selecting the Contra Voucher.**
7. **F5=To select the payment client.**
8. **F6=To select a Receipt Voucher.**
9. **F7=To select a Journal Voucher.**
10. **F8=To have a choice of Business Voucher.**
11. **Ctrl + F8=To select a Credit Note Voucher.**
12. **F9=To select any Purchase Voucher.**
13. **Ctrl + F9=To initiate Selection of Debit Note Voucher.**
14. **F10=To select any Reverse Journal Voucher.**
15. **Ctrl + F10=To initiate selection of Reminder Voucher.**
16. **F11=For selecting Screen Functions.**

17. **F12=To go to the Configuration Screen.**
18. **Alt + 2=To initiate use for Duplicate Voucher.**
19. **Alt + A=Adding the voucher to change to make a change in the center of the column report.**
20. **Alt + B=To check Outstanding balances.**
21. **Alt + C=To create a master on voucher screen (This will work only if you have not changed the function for the same).**
22. **Alt + D=To remove the Voucher or Delete the Master. Remove the table in the column report using this key.**
23. **Alt + E=For exporting the reports in ASCII, Excel, HTML, PDF, XML format.**
24. **Alt + I=To Insert Voucher/ Changes Between Items and Accounting.**
25. **Alt + G=For Selecting Language Configuration.**
26. **Alt + K=For making keyword configurations.**
27. **Alt + O=To Upload Reports.**
28. **Alt + G=To arrive at the Language Selection for Tally ERP 9.**
29. **Alt + M=For Deleting any message.**
30. **Alt + N=For Displaying Messages in Automatic Columns.**
31. **Alt + P=To initiate Printing of the Report.**
32. **Alt + R=For Removing Line from Report.**
33. **Alt + S=To check the Public Return of the Line Removed with Alt + R.**
34. **Alt + U=To Get the Last Used Line which was also removed before.**
35. **Alt + V=For Connecting invoice Screen with Stock Journals Screen.**
36. **Alt + X=To cancel Voucher in Daily List or Voucher List.**
37. **Alt + R=For Registering your Tally ERP 9.**
38. **Ctrl + B=For accommodation of Budget.**
39. **Ctrl + Alt + B=To Check the Statutory Details of the Company.**
40. **Ctrl + C=For choosing the Cost category.**
41. **Ctrl + E=To select any currency.**
42. **Ctrl + G=For selecting Group.**
43. **Ctrl + H=To take help from Help & Support Center.**

44. **Ctrl + I=For Selecting the Items in Stock.**
45. **Ctrl + Alt + I=For Implementation of Legal Masters.**
46. **Ctrl + K=For Logging in to Remote User Http://Tally.Net**
47. **Ctrl + L=For ledger selection.**
48. **Ctrl + O=For checking the Godowns in Tally Selection.**
49. **Ctrl + Q=The Screen exits and is left without Changes saved.**
50. **Ctrl + R=Helps you to Return directly to the Voucher Type.**
51. **Ctrl + Alt + R=To access the Company's Data.**
52. **Ctrl + S=To Change the Master of the Attack Items.**
53. **Ctrl + U=For Selecting any Unit.**
54. **Ctrl + V=To initiate Selection of Voucher Types and Wiring Between Billing and Goods.**
55. **Ctrl + K=For connecting directly to the Control Center.**
56. **Ctrl + H=To access the Help Center directly where You Can Send Questions Directly to the Tally erp9 developer and tally executives.**
57. **Alt + ENTER=To view the Voucher Display.**
58. **Alt + S=To forsee the Financial Report.**
59. **Alt + F1=For Detailed News.**
60. **Alt + F2=To Change the Period.**
61. **Alt + F3=To modify company information.**
62. **Alt + F4=To select the Trading order Type.**
63. **Alt + F5=For Selection of Sales order. Also, to gain Monthly and Quarterly display.**
64. **Alt + F6=For the selection of the order. To select or reject the voucher type.**
65. **Alt + F7=For Choosing an additional Vehicle Type to Accept all kind of Tests.**
66. **Alt + F8=For initiating the Display of Columnar Report.**
67. **Alt + F9=For the selection of External Paper Type.**
68. **Alt + F10=To select the Physical Vehicle Type.**
69. **Alt + F12=For filtering of Money Value information.**
70. **Alt + J=For the selection of Job Work Out Order Voucher.**
71. **Alt + W=For selecting Job Work in Order Voucher.**
72. **CTRL + A=For selecting a Form.**

73. **CTRL + N=To Switch to Calculator.**
74. **R=To generate ratio.**
75. **S=To look for stock.**
76. **P=To go to P&L.**
77. **B=To go to the Balance Sheet.**
78. **D + T=To go to Trial Balance.**
79. **E=For developing Order Voucher.**
80. **T=For developing Inventory Voucher.**
81. **Ctrl + Alt + F12=For going to Advanced Configuration.**
82. **PgUp=Helps Displaying the Previous Voucher When You Change the Voucher.**
83. **PgDn=Helps to display the Next Voucher While Changing the Voucher.**
84. **Esc + Enter=To Exit.**
85. **Q + Enter=For Quitting.**
86. **ENTER=To Accept Anything in a Field.**
87. **ESC=For Clearing the Entry.**
88. **Shift + ENTER=To Condense Next Level of Details.**
89. **CTRL + ENTER=To change the Master While Entering or Displaying a Message.**

GST Ready software shortcuts on Tally

1. **Alt + J=To get Statutory Adjustment Vouchers.**
2. **Alt + S=For availing Statutory Payment Voucher.**
3. **CTRL + O=For opening GST portal.**
4. **CTRL + E=To export any return.**
5. **CTRL + A=For viewing it accepted for as it is.**

What We Do?

Marg ERP Ltd. is a leader in the business software products arena. We specialise in Pharma & FMCG trade with over 50% market share in India. Since our inception in 1992, Marg's easy yet strong products have been revolutionizing the way businesses run in India & across the globe. Marg ERP Ltd is the leading provider of integrated business application software & apps for Micro, Small and Midsize Businesses. Marg ERP Ltd. is a Guinness World Record Holder, ISO Certified, CMMI Level 3 Company. Based on our best-of-breed offerings, we continue to build new alliances with industry leaders and win new customers across a range of major industries.

Three Fundamental Approaches For Achieving Milestones

Customer Centric Approach

Marg Customer-centric approach has always provided their customer with a positive customer experience before and after the sale of the software in order to drive repeat business and customer loyalty. We have spent years creating a culture around the customer and their needs. Marg Customers are Marg Family. We cater to every minute prospect of customer need to make their business journey easy & smooth.

Technology Oriented Approach

Marg does continuous research and development to build a long term relationship with partners & customers to nourish small & medium businesses across the globe. After rigorous research and consistent practice, we have designed Marg products using advanced technology with a talented bunch of individuals at our state of the art.

We ensure that software is updated with all the latest technology to provide a seamless experience to our valuable customers. Marg's primary goal is customer satisfaction and making India Digitally empowered.

Regular Innovation Approach

Marg's innovative approach focuses on new ideas and behaviours that significantly add to its business strategy, capability and market understanding. Marg is always committed to assure its regular services with value-added support. We always prefer to carry our legacy for the customer benefits and their happiness, therefore, reducing the gap between product & demands.

Marg's innovative approach focuses on new ideas and behaviours that significantly add to its business strategy, capability and market understanding. Marg is always committed to assure its regular services with value-added support. We always prefer to carry our legacy for the customer benefits and their happiness, therefore, reducing the gap between product & demands.

6

Marg Shortcut

Master

1. **Ledger =CTRL+L**
2. **Item =CTRL+I**
3. **Passwords & Powers =ALT+ALT+INSERT**

Transaction

1. **Create Sale=ALT+N**
2. **Create Challan=ALT+C, ALT+INSERT**
3. **Create Counter Sale=ALT+A**
4. **Modify Bill=ALT+M, CTRl+F3**
5. **Save Bill=TAB, END, CTRL+W**
6. **Create Purchase=ALT+P**

Accounts

1. **Voucher Entry=ALT+V**
2. **Single Entry=ALT+I**
3. **Cheques/Cash=ALT+U**
4. **P.D Cheques/Cash=ALT+Q**

Books

1. **All Ledgers=ALT+L, CTRL+L**
2. **Outstanding=ALT+O**

Hotkeys

1. **Search Menu=F11**
2. **Change User=CTRL+U**
3. **Data Entry=CTRl+F7**
4. **Bill Adjustment=CTRL+F9**
5. **Item List=CTRL+I**
6. **Calendar=Shift+F12**
7. **Calculator=F12**
8. **Personal Directory=CTRL+F1**
9. **Printer Setup=CTRL+F11**
10. **Switch Over=CTRL+J**
11. **Standard Narration=CTRL+F12**
12. **Quit=CTRL+Q**

7 Busy

1 What Is Busy Accounting Software?

- BUSY is a company accounting and management software for Micro, Small, and Medium Enterprises (MSMEs) (MSMEs). It is one of the most popular business accounting software in India, South Asia, the Middle East, and Africa, with over 400,000 licenses sold in over 20 countries.
- BUSY – company accounting software includes features such as full financial accounting, multi-location inventory, multi-currency, multi-tax capabilities, multi-branch management, order processing, payroll, MIS, Invoicing, and more, allowing you to make educated business decisions.
- BUSY is available in three distinct versions to meet the varying demands of MSMEs, namely Basic, Standard, and Enterprise, for enterprises of all sizes and types. BUSY may be utilized in practically all sorts of Business Segments and Industry Verticals, such as FMCG, Retail, Manufacturing, Trading, and Distribution because it is a horizontal product.
- BUSY is distributed and supported through a worldwide network of over 500 Channel Partners, hundreds of Resellers, and Solution Partners.

2 What Is The Price Of Busy Accounting Software?

- BUSY Accounting Software is available in four editions to meet the different business demands of Small and Medium Businesses: Express version is a completely free accounting program with limited but enough functionality for people who are just starting out in the company and only need the bare essentials. Invoicing, Accounting, Basic Inventory, and Statutory Reports are all included in the Basic package. It's designed for shops and small companies who need to keep track of their invoicing, bookkeeping, and compliance.
- The standard version is designed for medium-sized enterprises and includes a number of sophisticated features. It includes all of the features of the Basic version, as well as a number of additional business management capabilities such as Order / Quotation / Challan Management, Multiple Units of Items, Item Barcode / POS Billing, and more. Enterprise is designed for bigger businesses with several branches/locations or a high number of users that use BUSY.

3 How Simple Is It To Set Up And Utilize Busy Accounting Software?

- All deployment methods are supported by Busy Accounting Software, including cloud, SaaS, web-based, Android, Windows, and Windows.
- This program received a 4.5-star rating for simplicity of use from those who evaluated it.

4 Who Can Benefit From Busy Accounting Software?

- Busy accounting software caters to a variety of business kinds and sizes:
- Those who are just getting their firm off the ground and don't have many operational requirements.
- Basic functions like invoicing, basic inventory, bookkeeping, and statutory reporting can help shopkeepers and small enterprises.

- Appropriate for medium-sized organizations looking to boost productivity. It provides business management capabilities such as item barcode/POS billing, order/ quotation/ challan management, direct SMS/ email capability, and more, in addition to basic functionality.
- Also appropriate for large corporations with thousands of people working from many locations.
- It has enterprise features including customer service/inquiry management, multi-branch/location management, payroll administration, voucher approval system, and so on.

5 Shortcut Keys For Accounting Software?

- The following are some of the most often used Busy software shortcut keys for billing and account management:
- Ctrl+F3 – This shortcut will create a new voucher in any of the current day's ledgers.
- Make a payment: Add a payment record to a vendor ledger or a cash/bank account by pressing Ctrl+F5.
- Add a receipt record to any client ledger or cash/bank account by pressing Ctrl+F6.
- Using the F7 function key, you may repeat the values of your last entry while creating new entries with the same precise information.
- Calculator: F10 – While making any entry, use the F10 function key to activate the calculator.

In this article we will learn the Shortcut keys of the famous accounting software Busy, we have provided you the most useful shortcut keys that require while working on Busy Accounting Software, and also help you to perform a specific task much faster than that of the mouse. and you can download these shortcut keys in PDF and Excel files for future reference.

8

Busy Shortcut

1. **Alt/Ctrl+F1 = For Create New Ledger**
2. **Alt/Ctrl+F2 = For Create New Item**
3. **Alt+F3 = For Add All Vouchers Drop Down List**
4. **Alt + F4 = For Quit Busy (In Case Company should be Shut)**
5. **Alt/Ctrl+F5 = For Add New Payment Voucher**
6. **Alt/Ctrl+F6 = For Add New Receipt Voucher**
7. **Alt/Ctrl+F7 = For Add New Journal Voucher**
8. **Alt/Ctrl+F8 = For Add New Sales Voucher**
9. **Alt/Ctrl+F9 = For Add New Purchase Voucher**
10. **Alt + L = For Account Ledger (Summary)**
11. **Alt + I = For Item Monthly Summary**
12. **Alt/Ctrl +B = For Balance Sheet**
13. **Alt + M = For Modify Masters**
14. **Ctrl + T = For Trial Balance**
15. **Ctrl + A = For Account Ledger Monthly Summary**
16. **Ctrl + D = For Stock Items (with Party wise Details)**
17. **Ctrl + S = For Stock Status (Grouped wise Summary)**
18. **Alt + G = For GST Summary (with selecting period)**
19. **Alt +Ctrl +A =For Use Administration Features (In Case Open Any Report/voucher etc.)**
20. **Alt +Ctrl +D = For Use Display Features (In Case Open Any Voucher/Report etc.)**

21. **Ctrl + U = For Switch User**
22. **Ctrl + K =For Lock Program**
23. **Ctrl + F = For Configuration**
24. **Ctrl + R = For Account Receivable**
25. **Ctrl + P = For Account Payable**
26. **Ctrl/Alt+ X = For Voucher/Entry Cancel**
27. **Ctrl/Alt+ P = For Print Invoice/Ledger etc.**
28. **Alt + E = For Export Data**
29. **Alt + M = For Send Email**
30. **F5 = For List of Records (In case Voucher Feeding)**
31. **F2 = For Fast Way of Saving Voucher/Master**
32. **F3 = For Searching**
33. **F7 = For Using Filter**
34. **F9 = For Hide Entry**
35. **Alt + F9 = For Unhide Entry**
36. **F10 = For Open Calculator**
37. **F8 = For Delete Entry/Masters**
38. **F7 = For Repeat Last Task (Example: – Narration)**

9

Intuit QuickBooks

Developed by Intuit, QuickBooks is an accounting software whose products provide desktop and online accounting applications as well as cloud-based ones which can process bills and business payments. QuickBooks is mostly targeted at medium and small businesses. Ease of use and reporting functionality makes QuickBooks popular among these users.

Intuit has included many Web-based features in QuickBooks, including:

- Electronic payment functions
- Remote access capabilities
- Mapping features
- Remote payroll assistance and outsourcing
- Online banking and reconciliation
- Better mail functionality with Microsoft Outlook

QuickBooks also has help functions and other functionalities like pre-authorization of electronic funds and time tracking options for employees. A cloud solution called QuickBooks Online is also provided by Intuit in which the user can access the software with a secure logon by paying a subscription free. QuickBooks is upgraded and updated on a regular basis by Intuit.

Even for business owners and users who lack financial or accounting background, QuickBooks is generally considered easy to use and understand. Another benefit of QuickBooks is in the availability of ready-to-use templates to create charts, business plans, invoices and spreadsheets. It can also help save time and effort for business owners by automating their signatures (which is scanned and uploaded for use) on business checks. Integration with other applications is also a big advantage of QuickBooks. It has a user-friendly interface and can guide users through each of its features.

Although QuickBooks is one of the most widely used brands of accounting software, some other brands of software are considered to provide more transparency in calculations, better audit trails, lesser upgrade fees and better deletion history than QuickBooks.

10

Intuit QuickBooks Shortcuts

Learn keyboard shortcuts for doing things more efficiently in QuickBooks Desktop for Windows and Mac.

You can use keyboard shortcuts to do all kinds of things in QuickBooks Desktop. Instead of using the menus, you can create invoices and move between windows with just a few keystrokes.

Note: You'll see underlined letters on some forms and buttons. These are shortcut labels. To use the shortcut, hold Alt and press the underlined letter.

Intuit QuickBooks Keyboard Shortcuts Windows

(Pro, Premier, Enterprise)

Navigate around QuickBooks

1. **Open the Help window=F1**
2. **Close current window=Esc**

3. **Open the Product Information window (Product and License number, company file location, etc)=F2 or Ctrl + 1**
4. **Open the Find Transaction window (Transactions, invoices, etc)=Ctrl + F**
5. **Open the Search window (Customers, accounts, transactions, etc)=F3 or Ctrl + 2**
6. **Open Tech Help / Technical Info window (System info)=F2 to open the Product Info window, then press F3**

Data fields on forms

1. **Increase or decrease the amount=+ or -**
2. **Go to the next data field=Tab**
3. **Go to the previous data field=Shift + Tab**
4. **Copy, paste, undo, cut=Ctrl + C, Ctrl + V, Ctrl + Z, Ctrl + X**
5. **Open calendar to select a date=Alt + ▾**
6. **Advance a day=+**
7. **Back a day=-**
8. **Go to today=T**
9. **Go to the first day of the week=W**
10. **Go to the last day of the week=K**
11. **Go to the same day next week=]**
12. **Go to the same day last week=[**
13. **Go to the first day of the month =M**
14. **Go to the last day of the month=H**
15. **Go to the same day of the month next month=;**
16. **Go to the same day of the month last month=' (apostrophe)**
17. **Go to the first day of the year (Jan 1)=Y**

Forms and transactions (invoices, expenses, etc)

1. **Record or save a transaction=Enter**
2. **Add a new transaction line=Ctrl + Ins**
3. **Delete selected transaction line=Ctrl + Del**
4. **Copy a transaction line=Highlight a transaction line, then press Ctrl + Alt + Y. *Only available in QuickBooks 2018 and later.**
5. **Paste a transaction line=Highlight a blank transaction line, then press Ctrl + Alt + V. *Only available in QuickBooks 2018 and later.**
6. **Go to the next or previous transaction line=▴ or ▾**
7. **Open the full list for the selected dropdown menu (product, service, customer, etc)=Highlight the ▼ dropdown menu, then press Ctrl + L. Press Ctrl + U to add a selected item from the list to your open form.**
8. **Move between pages on forms and reports=Page Up or Page Down**
9. **Save and close the current form=Alt + S**
10. **Go to your last open form of the same type=Alt + P**
11. **Save and go to the next form of the same type=Alt + N**
12. **Print form (or list)=CTRL + P**
13. **Memorize current form and its transactions=Ctrl + M**
14. **Open Memorized Transaction List=Ctrl + T**
15. **Open transaction history (for current form)=Ctrl + H**
16. **Open transaction journal (for current form)=Ctrl + Y**

Lists (Customer Center, Account Register, Item List, etc)

1. **Go to the first item or last item on a list or register=Ctrl + Page Up or Ctrl + Page Down**
2. **Create a new item on a list (account, customer, product or service, etc)=Ctrl + N**

3. **Edit an item on a list (account, customer, product or service, etc)=Ctrl + E**
4. **Delete an item on a list (account, customer, product or service, etc)=Ctrl + D**
5. **Run a Quick Report for an item on a list=Ctrl + F6**
6. **Refresh list (You only see this if you are in the multi-user mode. This is useful if multiple users are editing the same list.)=F5**

Start a new task anywhere in QuickBooks

1. **Create a new invoice=Ctrl + I**
2. **Create a new check=Ctrl + W**
3. **Open the Customer Center=Ctrl + J**
4. **Open the Chart of Accounts=Ctrl + A**
5. **Open an Account Register=Ctrl + R, then select an account. If you are in an account register, select a transaction and press Ctrl+G. This opens the register for the associated "transfer" account.**

Open, set up, and close QuickBooks

1. **Open your company file with no open windows or menus=Hold Alt after you open your company file on the Open Company window**
2. **Close QuickBooks=Alt + F4**
3. **Open QuickBooks Service Keys (Payroll only)=Ctrl + K**
4. **Set up YTD Amounts for Payroll (Payroll only)=Select the Help menu and then About QuickBooks. When the product screen appears, Ctrl + Alt + Y.**

Intuit QuickBooks Shortcuts For Mac

Navigate around QuickBooks

1. **Open the Help window=Command + ?**
2. **Minimize current window=Command + M**
3. **Open Preferences=Command + , (comma)**
4. **Open the Product Information window (Product and License number, company file location, etc)=Command + 1**
5. **Open the Find Transaction window (Transactions, invoices, etc)=Command + F**
6. **Hide QuickBooks =Command + H**

Data fields on forms

1. **Go to the next data field=Tab**
2. **Go to the previous data field=Shift + Tab**
3. **Copy, paste, undo, cut=Command + C, Command + V, Command + Z, Command + X**
4. **Increase or decrease the check or form number by one=+ or -**
5. **Delete the character to the left=Delete**

Date fields on forms

1. **Advance a day=+**
2. **Back a day=-**
3. **Go to today=T**

4. **Go to the first day of the week=W**
5. **Go to the last day of the week=K**
6. **Go to the first day of the month=M**
7. **Go to the last day of the month=H**
8. **Go to the first day of the year (Jan 1)=Y**
9. **Go to the last day of the year (Dec 31)=R**

Forms and transactions (invoices, expenses, etc)

1. **Add a new transaction line=Command + Y**
2. **Delete selected transaction line=Command + B**
3. **Open the full list for the selected dropdown menu (product, service, customer, etc)=Highlight the ▼ dropdown menu, then press Command + L**
4. **Move between pages on forms and reports=FN + ▴ or ▾**
5. **Print form (or list)=Command + P**
6. **Memorize current form and its transactions=Command and + (plus)**
7. **Open transaction history (for current form)=Command + U**

Lists (Customer Center, Account Register, Item List, etc)

1. **Create a new item on a list (account, customer, product or service, etc)=Command + N**
2. **Edit an item on a list (account, customer, product or service, etc)=Command + E**
3. **Delete an item on a list (account, customer, product or service, etc)=Command + D**
4. **Open an Account Register=Command + R, then select an account**

Start a new task anywhere in QuickBooks

1. **Create a new invoice=Command + I**
2. **Create a new check=Command + K**
3. **Open the transaction journal=Command + T**
4. **Open the Chart of Accounts=Shift + Command + A**
5. **Open the Customer Center=Shift + Command + J**
6. **Open the Employee Center=Shift + Command + E**
7. **Open the Item list=Shift + Command + I**
8. **Open the Memorized Transactions list=Shift + Command + M**
9. **Open the Vendor Center=Shift + Command + V**

Open, set up, and close QuickBooks

1. **Open a company file=Command + O**

WHAT IS ZOHO BOOKS?

- Zoho Books is your one-stop platform for managing your accounting tasks and organizing your transactions. It's a single secure location to keep up with your company's bills and invoices, reconcile your bank statements, control your spending, oversee projects, and eliminate GST compliance worries.

Zoho Books is future ready. Are you?

- Keeping up with the market means understanding ever-changing business trends, taxes, cloud implementations, and more. Zoho Books helps you stay current, from customizing your accounting to understanding your income well-being and everything in between.

Zoho Books is our user's first choice because we put them first
Usability

- Zoho Books' clean and simple dashboard gives you immediate, convenient insight into your financial health. An effective, user-friendly UI makes Zoho Books easy to navigate.

Security

- Zoho Books protects your privacy and security with IP restrictions, two-factor authentication, SSL, and more. Your data can only be accessed by the users that you authorize. Learn more about Zoho's privacy and security policy.

Extensibility

- Zoho Books is designed to help your business connect across multiple platforms. Extend your accounting with a library of more than 300 business apps via Zapier, or take advantage of built-in connections with other apps in the Zoho suite.

Reliability

- Zoho Books is built with dependable features that protect your data and produce accurate results for your accounting. Rely on Zoho Books' customer support team to assist you in making the best use of Zoho Books.

12

Zoho Books Shortcuts

Keyboard shortcuts / hotkeys enable you to use Zoho Books with ease and convenience. You can instantly perform actions within the application using the keyboard shortcuts.

Note: Press Shift + ? to instantly view the shortcut keys in a pop-up while using Zoho Books.

If you forget where to look for your shortcut keys, you can always click the help icon in the top-right corner and click

Keyboard Shortcuts to view them!

The shortcuts in Zoho Books are categorized based on the pages in which you can use the shortcut keys. Let's look into how they are categorized.

General

You can use these shortcuts from anywhere in the organization and they would take you to the respective page or perform the particular action.

Say, you are looking into the Balance Sheet of an organization and you would like to quickly navigate another organization of yours. You can just press **o** in your keyboard from any module to view the list of organizations you have in Zoho Books.

Likewise, the following actions are common to all modules:

1. / =Jump to the Search Bar. Search by modules or click Advanced Search to drill down all details.
2. s =Open your Settings page in the current window.
3. o =Navigate to your list of Organizations in Zoho Books.

Go To Actions

You can use the following shortcut keys to navigate to a specific tab. These could be the most common actions you perform in your day-to-day accounting activity.

1. Shift+i =Just like the General Shortcuts, these actions are also common to all the modules. They are:
2. Shift+e =Jump to the the Invoices tab.
3. Shift+n =Jump to the the Estimates tab.
4. Shift+b =Jump to the the Credit Notes tab.
5. Shift+b =Jump to the the Bills tab.

6. Shift+x =Jump to the the Expense tab.
7. Shift+p =Jump to the the Purchase Orders tab.
8. Shift+s =Jump to the the Sales Orders tab.
9. Shift+a =Jump to the the Chart of Accounts tab.

Module Level Actions

Once you've navigated to a particular module, you can use the following shortcut keys to perform actions specific to a particular module (Example:Invoices/Bills). These shortcuts are applicable only to the Sales and Purchase entities.

Let's say you are planning to move all data from one organization to another and the Module Level Actions let's you complete them really quick! Click **alt+e** to export data from one organization and click **alt+i** in your other organization to import files

1. n =Create a New Transaction.
2. alt+m =Email all/multiple transactions from the same module.
3. alt+p =Print all/multiple transactions from the same module.
4. alt+d =Download all/multiple transactions from the same module as a PDF.
5. alt+i =Import all data to a particular module from your computer.
6. alt+e =Export all data from a particular module to your computer.
7. alt+a =Select all transactions in a specific module
8. shift+mouse left key =Select all transactions between two intervals.

Transaction Level Actions

After you have selected a transaction, you can use the following shortcut keys to perform actions at the transaction level. The following shortcuts let you perform actions quickly without having to reach for a mouse. These shortcuts are applicable only to the Sales and Purchase entities.

1. e =Edit an existing transaction.
2. m =Mail a transaction.
3. p =Print a transaction.
4. d =Download transactions as a PDF.
5. alt+s =Save transactions when you create them.
6. alt+p =Save and Print a transaction.

Creation Actions

What are keyboard shortcuts for if they don't let you create transactions in a flash? The following shortcuts will help you create new transactions across various modules from anywhere in the organization.

1. c+i =Create a new Invoice.
2. c+e =Create a new Estimate.
3. c+n =Create a new Credit Note.
4. c+b =Create a new Bill.
5. c+x =Create a new Expense.
6. c+p =Create a new Purchase Order.
7. c+s =Create a new Sales Order.
8. c+a =Create a new Account in your Chart of Accounts.

13 ProfitBooks

#1 FREE Accounting Software
For Your Business.

ProfitBooks helps you to stay on top of business finances without any accounting knowledge.

""After evaluating almost 10 different software, we finally bought ProfitBooks and it turned out to be the best decision for our business.""

– Mark Somers, Jackster Corp.

Manage Your Money Without Accounting Knowledge

Designed for business owners who want to keep their finances in order!

ProfitBooks is fastest growing & amazingly simple to use online accounting software. It lets you create beautiful invoices, track expenses and manage inventory without any accounting knowledge..

You can easily share the transaction data with your accountant. Know whats going on with your business with just few clicks & take better decisions.

Grow Your Sales With Powerful Invoicing

Get paid on time and maintain positive cash flow.

With ProfitBooks accounting software, you can create professional estimates or invoices and track outstanding payments due with few clicks.

- Create beautiful invoices
- Receive online payments using payment gateway
- Record advance payments
- Track accounts receivables with sales reports

Track Inventory With Ease

From Purchase To Sales, Track Entire Inventory Lifecycle

Whether you are manufacturing, distributing, selling, servicing, or just managing the inventory, ProfitBooks can handle all your business processes with ease.

- Simplify purchase workflow with POs
- Track manufacturing processes
- Maintain product batches
- Track inventory flow at multiple warehouses
- Easily find low stock using powerful reports

Run Your Business With Total Confidence

From financial accounting to tax compliance, ProfitBooks makes everything easy for your business.

ProfitBooks is the best bookkeeping solution for your business. Apart from recording income & expense, you can record journal entries and manage taxes.

- Generate detailed tax reports
- Colloborate with your accountant online

- Record manual journals
- Track business expenses

Remote Bookkeeping Service

Don't have time for accounting? Let us handle it for you!

Our team of expert accountants will help you with accounting & tax filing. All you have to do is to send your bank statement, invoices & expense bills to us and your dedicated bookkeeper will do the rest.

- Always on-time tax filing
- Up to date bookkeeping of all transactions
- Monthly reporting of financial performance
- Call with expert accountants to address queries

Printed by Libri Plureos GmbH in Hamburg,
Germany